Minnesota State Fair

Deep Fried Thoughts on Cheese Curds, Carnies, and The Human Condition

By Ben Nesvig

Acknowledgements

Special thanks to:
- You for reading this
- The great people of Minnesota for creating a memorable experience worthy of publication
- My wife for being an eager participant in my quest for food at the State Fair and for taking photos of it all
- Caroline Lyngstad for serving as Advising Editor
- Kaia Boal (http://exhibit-k.com/) for designing the book cover
- Mothers with Kindles across America

Copyright

"Poets have been mysteriously silent on the subject of cheese."
- G.K. Chesterton, Philosopher

Welcome To The Fair

It has been roughly 18 hours since I've eaten anything of substance.

Am I on a deserted island, journaling my final hours onto scraps of paper among the scattered remains of a shipwrecked boat?

Far from it.

I'm with my wife and 50 other Minnesotans of all shapes and sizes in an accordion city bus, heading east-bound for the Minnesota State Fair. The rows of the bus are filled with the entire spectrum of society—elderly sitting in stoic silence, adults occasionally leaning into their spouse to whisper, "Let's remember to get a bucket of cookies this year" and little kids beaming happiness with their permanent smiles as we approach Minnesota's version of Disneyland. And there is me.

I'm standing in the aisle, legs outstretched and knees bent for balance, with my right hand clasping a metal fireman's pole. The bus sways onto the shoulder of the highway, bypassing rush hour traffic. The bus' air conditioning is waging a battle against the Minnesota heat. The beads of congregating sweat on the small of my back tally up a victory for the humidity over this communal shuttle to the State Fair. A whiff of bus exhaust graces my nostrils only to be pushed aside by the muffled cough-inducing stench of the man standing next to me. Despite being nauseous and pumping out sweat from all pores, I couldn't be more excited.

The Minnesota State Fair, otherwise known as "The Great Minnesota Get-Together" happens once a year near the end of August, spanning 12 days through Labor Day weekend. From mini donuts to butter carvings to beer gardens to animal barns, the world is your deep fried oyster at the Minnesota State Fair.

The bus sneaks onto the shoulder of the highway as we crawl past lines of traffic-stalled cars full of miserable people likely on their way home from work instead of being on this Hajj to Minnesota's greasy Mecca. Only a few more miles before I devour one of my favorite days of the year.

It's impossible for me to enter the State Fair without a mental checklist. It helps soothe the fear and anxiety my taste buds have of missing out. I'll cross the threshold of the State Fair carrying nothing but a mental checklist, a wallet full of fresh ATM cash, and a childlike giddiness to devour things that exist far outside the food pyramid. "Items to consume" are as follows (or, if I'm not alive when you're reading this, consider it a coroner's "cause of death" report):

- Cheese curds
- Grilled corn on the cob
- Deep fried cookie dough
- Strawberry milkshake from the Dairy Barn

Everything else is icing on this constipation cake. Man was not built to handle a tornado of grease, butter, cheese, and sugar, but that's what I'm pummeling my digestive system with today. Maybe we'll also get to pet some animals. The Minnesota State Fair is my one opportunity each year to get up close and mingle with a few exotic animals, like goats and sheep.

Like a moth to a flame and a Minnesotan to hot dish, I feel pulled here by something primal, something so innate it eludes conscious definition. Yes, I want cheese curds. Yes, I want a strawberry milkshake. Yes, I want to eat so much my belt files for unemployment and my pants become tights. I enjoy these indulgences, but I also enjoy spending an air conditioned evening at home with a ham sandwich and a good book.

Why do I come to the State Fair every year without fail? Have I been enslaved by Lady Cheese Curd's greasy golden seduction? While I get a thrill out of the food, I'd just be as comfortable eating a shameful amount of fried delicacies at a Chinese buffet without an audience of a hundred thousand strangers watching me wipe butter off my face. What exactly has led me to the State Fair over two dozen times since my birth? The unanswered question of *why* bothers me, like the last remaining ounce of a milkshake that refuses to be slurped into the straw. I need resolve.

The bus finally grinds to a stop at our destination on Como Avenue in St. Paul. The door between me and glutton heaven opens with a dramatic "GUSSSH." I mumble a distracted but appreciative "thanks" to the bus driver as I walk hand in sweaty hand with my wife to the pearly gates of the Minnesota State Fair.

I give my admission ticket to the elderly State Fair worker resting on a folding chair. A bead of sweat barrels down my outstretched arm, a gross reminder of the humidity. The elderly worker hastily rips my ticket and gives close to half of it back, along with a smile and permission to enter. Slogging into the crowd with this thick humidity feels like walking through someone's mouth. What drives me to endure this misery? So begins my search for meaning—but first, deep fried cheese.

Cheese Curds

Cheese curds are the Grand Canyon of food—people can tell you all about it, but you just have to experience it yourself to truly grasp the raw, magnificent beauty. Both are responsible for a few accidental deaths each year, I assume.

Cheese is usually nothing to write home about—it's just a humble addition to other foods, content being the bridesmaid and never the bride, yet its mere presence makes the taste of everything far superior than before. Apple slices, crackers, shavings of salami—all mediocre without the presence of cheese. But today the cheese is on the altar and now it's time to consummate the marriage of cheese and grease.

Though the cheese curd is deep fried, providing a unique crunchy texture, the ingredients are simple: Cheese, batter, and a testament to a complete lack of willpower. And not just my willpower, but all those who attend the State Fair—over 100,000 pounds of cheese curds are devoured by State Fair goers every year. I'm not a nutritionist, but I know cheese curds are the most delicious way to have a heart attack. Seven out of five doctors agree, as likely do all consumers of the aforementioned 100,000 pounds of breathtaking cheese.

Walking into the Food Building, I'm nervous with excitement and get into line (of course, there is a line. If there wasn't a line, it'd be a poor reflection upon the good state of Minnesota). The line is moving quickly, thanks to its simple ordering process. The only two options customers have are the size of the cheese curd order and a drink. What a relief.

I love having the freedom to choose, I just hate the complexity and burden of choice. I never know which option is better and then worry I'll have wasted a trip when everyone except me knew option B was obviously superior. I never know which option is better—inevitably, it turns out to be whatever selection I didn't make, so the time I spend agonizing over my options is wasted. Last month while visiting a local deli for the first time and carefully weighing the possibilities presented on the menu, I ordered a salad. The cashier responded, "You don't want a salad. They're not good here. Get something else." With freedom to choose comes freedom to fail. Because of the streamlined options at the cheese curd stand, this food order is the most enjoyable conundrum I've had the pleasure to suffer in months.

"Large cheese curds," I plead to the young teen, towering over me in the raised cheese curd hut. I don't enjoy when businesses do this, raising the platform for their cashiers. Ordering from the cashier on the raised platform makes me feel like I'm taking orders from a judge with my conscious as the jury and the cheese curds executioner of my arteries. I present him a five dollar bill before he even requests payment—no point in taking baby steps across the finish line. Before he even deposits my money into the cash drawer, I'm holding a paper basket of battered and deep fried mozzarella goodness. Hallelujah.

"AHHH! AUGHHHH!!!" I sputter while tossing the volcano of cheese back and forth in my mouth in attempt to cool it down. "They're hot?" my wife asks, already knowing the answer, but perhaps only verifying I hadn't caused myself permanent injury. She knows full well what to expect on this cheese curd carousel I hop on every year. Despite the scorched mouth, I'm in a state of careless satisfaction. I don't need the skin on the roof of my mouth. If anything, it will just make the milkshake from the Dairy Barn taste that much more refreshing, enabling a new layer of raw skin to get some ice cream action. Nothing can derail this food devouring train that's now in motion.

"I can't eat any more," the wife sighs, after wisely waiting for the cheese to cool, and selecting just a few curds to eat, despite our tacit agreement that, as man and wife, we split everything 50/50. The truth is that she generally peters out around 35%. That leaves us with a lonely trio of curds.

"Ok," I reply, casually liberating her of the 50/50 split chains, maintaining my poker face on the outside while feeling the joy of a little kid on Halloween who can't stop eating his candy. I could easily throw away the last remaining cheese curds, but I can't bring myself to actually do it. Sure, I could quit eating, but I was raised in a society where if you didn't clean your plate, you were basically giving the middle finger to a kid in Africa. Finishing my food is hardwired into my thinking.

You can only eat so many cheese curds before they congregate in the stomach, holding hands, singing "We wish you a merry constipation." But today, I am triumphant. Fortune is with me, as I was able to finish off all the curds before my digestive system is crushed beneath the combined weight of my consumption and guilt. Today, I will not be remorseful about how much I eat, unlike when I choose to eat two donuts for lunch and a cupcake for dinner, which is a situation I only wish was hypothetical. Tossing the empty cheese curd container in the trash, I'm filled with pride—you're not truly an American until you can be embarrassed by how much food you've consumed.

"Where should we go next?" my wife asks. A new craving hits my taste buds and I answer, "Corn dog." It may increase my pride or my shame, maybe both. I need to find out, pronto.

Pronto Pup

Just as America isn't Canada, the Pronto Pup isn't a corn dog, but slightly better (I can say this because I love maple syrup and no one from Canada is going to read this, so settle down). The corn dog is a hot dog wrapped in a layer of cornmeal presented on a stick. The corn dog, as the name suggests, is made with cornmeal. The Pronto Pup, in contrast, is a mix of batter and unicorn tears. Okay, so I have no idea what the Pronto Pup made of, but it's something magical and I prefer not knowing. When it comes to food, surprise ingredients never work in the consumer's favor. Staggering in its length, the Papa Pup is the comically expanded version of the Pronto Pup, more so resembling a child's baseball bat than a corn dog.

With exact change in hand and an admirable spring in my step, I approach the Pronto Pup container. "One Papa Pup," I say, pushing money onto the cashier with unnecessary enthusiasm. "Oh," the man says, suddenly crestfallen, putting down the regular-sized Pronto Pup he had prepared with my approach. Do I inform him that this purchase is to share with my wife (i.e., I'm not a complete animal)? No, that might make things awkward, so I simply stare in awed silence as I observe him and his craft. Like an artist, he brushes the perfect amount of ketchup onto this culinary masterpiece—enough to glaze, but not so much that it drips onto my exposed, flip flop-wearing feet. He hands the Papa Pup to me. I accept it with delicate grace, as if being handed a newborn.

A few exchanged bites of the footlong Papa Pup bring up the food on a stick dilemma. First bite? Glorious. Second bite? Satisfaction. Third and fourth bites? Easy. Everything after? Awkward. The Papa Pup has to be the longest food-on-a-stick item at the fair. Unlike a popsicle, where after a few bites you can press the wooden stick into your cheek, grasping the bottom of the popsicle with your teeth, pulling up the remaining popsicle like a helicopter rescuing a deserted man at sea, it's almost impossible to eat a Papa Pup after a few bites. Instead of a rounded edge like a popsicle stick, the Papa Pup is on a soft wooden spear, perhaps the only shape that could penetrate the infinite inches of hot dog.

A couple of bites into the Papa Pup, I can either attempt to continue my course of action, biting from the head at any angle, or I can push up the hot dog up from the bottom, inching it toward judgment day.

If I went head on, I'd be attempting to swallow a wooden sword, risking a soft poke to the back of my neck, inducing the gag reflex. I'm content to suffer a little pain, whether physical or emotional, in exchange for consuming feel-good food, but I can't this time. My irrational fear of dying while eating ridiculous food has just been triggered. Whenever someone dies, 1). sympathies are exchanged, then 2). the question "How did it happen?" is posed. I don't ever want that question to be answered like this: "Ben died as a result of shoving a Papa Pup down his throat. At least he passed doing what he loved. Ben is survived by family members who wish to remain anonymous."

I choose to push the hot dog up from the bottom. The Papa Pup is stubborn. The feeble attempt to hoist the hot dog up the stick only squishes the Papa Pup, resulting in what looks like a deformed caterpillar stuck mid lunge.

The wife and I nibble off the rest, sinking into the muscle memory of eating ribs because there was no other way to attack this situation. What remains of the Papa Pup is a stick that wouldn't clear security at the airport and could easily kill a vampire. Heaving the wooden javelin into the trash before I accidentally trip and poke my eye out, we search for a place to rest our stomachs.

Remembering that binge eating is a marathon and not a sprint, we begin walking toward the closest building, led by the smell of manure toward the promise of animals.

The Chickens Are Restless

Chickens. Rows and rows... of clucking chickens. For those who've never been to the Poultry building, two important things: 1). The public isn't allowed to pet the chickens. The sign mandating this is a little presumptuous since I've never felt the urge in my entire life to touch, pet, or poke a chicken, but now I'm running a mental simulation of what would happen if I pet one of the chickens. 2). If you can't easily tune out distracting noises, you'll swear that you're walking through a torture chamber. Nails across a mile-long chalkboard would be a sweet release from the audible terror of a hundred chickens.

It is to this soundtrack that I allow my mind to wander as I wait for my stomach to settle. I like the idea of owning a chicken as a pet—not for companionship, but for pumping out a few eggs each day for my breakfast. And if an intruder ever enters my home, the eggs can just as quickly transform into a weapon. Of all the types of birds one can own as a pet, the chicken makes the most sense to me. Chickens work as an alarm clock, egg producer, and way to train for a karate competition (at least in movies). I'd also settle for a penguin. The fact that my two favorite birds either can't fly or not very well may suggest I have issues with abandonment.

Do I have issues with abandonment? And is this epiphany driven by self-awareness or is it disappointment and regret driven by the tortured clucking I hear in stereo, or the eye-stinging power of chicken excrement? Cackle. Cackle. Which is it? Cluck. Cluck. And what can the chickens possibly be trying to communicate with this squawking? The incessant noise piercing my ears must be why humans started eating chickens—just to get them to shut the cluck up.

As we exit the barn, a group of people are hovering over a handful of rabbits in a cage. Before I can join in the chorus of "Awww, adorable!" I notice a sign next to the rabbits indicating what the most popular types of rabbit meat are. Why would someone gazing upon this cage of helpless creatures wonder, "What are the most celebrated ways to feast upon an animal like this?" And how does this inquiry come up so often that it warrants a sign? The sign does only one thing for me: It confirms I need to exit the poultry barn.

Life Lesson Droppings

Food? Rides? The Grand Stand? Too many choices! I pull out a map that an enthusiastic woman lady gave me on the way in, scanning it in search of something worth exerting the minimal effort of walking. Let's see, according to this map... I have no idea where I am. There are no helpful "You are here" signs. I'm lost without them and technology, upon which I am entirely dependent for movement, like an old man with his prunes.

I can't read a map without it showing "You Are Here" or robotically commanding turn-by-turn directions. I can no longer get in my car and just calmly drive to my destination. I need the emotional support of my GPS. I go through the trouble of punching the address into my phone even if I already know the route. This is so I can focus on important things during my commute—such as being amazed by how many people eat while they drive. Also, technology provides me an alibi for tardiness. "Sorry, the phone took me on some strange route that coincidentally took me past my favorite cupcake place, which is why I'm late. Stupid phone."

As I hold the map in my hands and try to sort out my State Fair future, I capture unusual movement out of the corner of my eye. Turning my head, I observe a middle-aged man leaping into the air, one foot following the other like a ballerina dancing across a lake of horse poop. After landing, he gives a quick peek to each of his shoes, scanning for manure. Evidently declaring success, he continues his journey to the end of a long line for a fruit smoothie.

I've witnessed something profound here. I can learn from this. Everyone wants something in life, but only those who are willing to go through the crap that stands in their way will be successful. The man vaulting steaming piles of generous horse droppings had to work for his smoothie and I'm positive it tasted better to him than someone who just moseyed on into the line from a dung-free path. I continue to watch the man standing in line and wonder, "Should I share this horse poop meaning of life theory with him?" After some contemplation, I decide against it. No one wants to talk about crap with strangers.

Just then, I see a young boy trailing behind his father down the poop-strewn street. Eyes fixed upon his father next to him, he is oblivious to the impending danger—his right foot is just about to sink into a steaming pile of turds. His knee bends and he extends his foot, it's all happening right before my eyes in tragic slow motion. All synapses are firing in my brain, but my lips are too slow to scream the warning, "NOOOOOOOOOOOO!!!" But just in the nick of time, his father grabs the back of his son's shirt, lifting him up and off the ground. Saved!

The boy's shoes will remain clean today. But what about that one day his father isn't around to mind his child's feet? What then? In this life, if you don't watch your step, you're going to end up in crap. Who knows, maybe we all end up in crap at one time or another as we hopscotch through an existence fraught with trials and tribulations. Maybe the point is that we all end up confronting crap, but if we're lucky, we'll be able to leap over it with grace instead of stepping into - and carrying - it with us wherever we go.

I've thought far too much about this subject.

Grandstand

We enter a large, brick two-story building, home to a variety of foods and a mixed bag of vendors with no commonality other than their shared desire to alleviate the grazing crowd of their money. Slogging up the long inclined walkway to the Grandstand entrance provides the most intense exercise I'll receive all day. I can't decipher if the salty discharge streaming down my forehead is sweat or food guilt being washed away, but the exertion feels productive.

As we enter, my eyes bounce in every direction to keep up with the stimulus—the variety, excitement and the potential of it all is overwhelming. Within ten steps of the entrance, I can purchase a circular plastic widget to corral and organize long extension cords, and at the next booth I can pick up informational pamphlets about Islam. What I'll find around the corner is unpredictable—it could be a vendor selling umbrellas that glow in the dark, or a jolly, kilt clad German peddling sausages.

Anything that is possible is probable here. That's why we (me and the thousands of people who voluntarily decided to squish into this building with me) enjoy a stroll through the Grandstand. The foods at the State Fair are mostly predictable, with the exception of a handful of new, well-publicized foods for anyone who is curious, but the Grandstand is a mystery. This is why I am drawn to this building despite the lack of desire to actually buy something—curiosity, wonder, and the hope of a better future, thanks to German sausages.

That curiosity, wonder, and hope is snuffed when I turn the corner—in the middle of a crowd, a man with the charisma of a magician is demonstrating flameless candles. What a letdown! I like flameless candles, but it's another step forward with the imitation society, where everything is becoming a bubble-wrapped replica of what it is supposed to be. One by one, I've witnessed these imitations gain acceptance into mainstream society as substitutions for their originals, and it breaks my organic heart. The chickenless chicken nuggets. The milkless milk. The meatless meatloaf. The "I Can't Believe It's Not Butter" butter. It's another reminder that we do to products what we do to ourselves—substitute what makes us unique with what makes us feel safe.

We as a society have embraced flameless candles because they make it impossible to burn the house down. Is this a fair trade when flameless candles give us a tenth of the joy actual candles do? As a child, running my index finger back and forth through the flame of a candle, occasionally wincing in pain, was exhilarating (still exhilarating as an adult). It was a way to test my limits.

I'm now hungry to exit the Grandstand to test the limits of what I can eat.

Deep Fried Cookie Dough

A wave of mini donut goodness tickles my nostrils, rewarding me for returning to the open air outside the Grandstand. Where is that glorious scent coming from? To where can I respond to the desire summoning me? A subtle smile spreads upon my face as I dreamily follow where my nose directs me, letting the aroma flood my mind with images of mini-donuts sweeping me off my feet. Where did that smell come from? I know of only one place at the State Fair that exclusively sells mini donuts, but the smell seems to travel further than anything else.

I come to an unexpected halt when an older gentleman, who I must have been following too closely, just stops. No warning—*NONE!*—just a "I don't know where I'm going so I'm just going to slam on the brakes, as if I weren't surrounded by thousands of people. I will act genuinely surprised, if I choose to acknowledge at all, that my actions single-handedly caused complete chaos" maneuver.

I decide to zigzag around him, summoning agility I was unaware I possessed. As we make our way back into the roaming masses on the streets, my wife suggests we share deep fried cookie dough. Despite devotion to a mini donut quest just moments earlier, I quickly agree to this culinary conquest. I adore cookie dough. Whenever I open the refrigerator at home to discover recently purchased cookie dough, I try to express indifference, as if I could will that indifference onto myself. "Oh. Cookie dough. How interesting," I remark playing hard to get. Several hours later, I'm wearing a winter coat in the middle of summer because I've spent the entire day in front of the open refrigerator, slowly chiseling away at that precious block of fine eatery.

The deep fried cookie dough is presented as three balls on a stick. The entire history of civilization indicates that three is the perfect amount. Three blind mice. Three wise men. Three Stooges. Three Musketeers. Three men and a baby. Third degree burns on the roof of my mouth from cheese curds. Three deep fried cookie dough balls on a stick. And in the not too distant future, I assume, triple bypass surgery.

Taking my first bite of one of the cookie dough balls liberates it from the stick. The remainder of the lone nugget screams "FREEEEEEEEDOM!" as it plops onto the tin foil that the cookie dough balls on a stick came in. The remaining cookie dough balls are barely hanging on, sagging from the stick like a bloated plastic grocery bag. As I begin to chew, the blast of sugar and chocolate jolts awake every taste bud in my mouth. The warm cookie dough tastes as if someone pulled cookies from the oven ten minutes before they were done baking, deep fried them, and then sprinkled powdered sugar on top, possibly in attempt to kill me with pleasure. With the second bite, the emotional brain has officially pummeled any rational decision making to a gooey pulp. The emotions are drunk on sugar behind my greasy wheel of thought, driving me toward the only destination they know—regret.

The wife and I exchange bites back and forth until there is just one cookie dough ball left. "I'm done," she says. As ecstasy-inducing as this has been, unfortunately, I'm done too. This is a situation.

I hate wasting food. My entire life, I've been raised to not waste food. When I was a kid, the only clubs that existed were the "Clean Plate Club" and the "No Girls Allowed Club" which I remained a member of for far longer than I care to mention. Today having a clean plate generally means you're fat, or at least on a one-way road toward that destination.

Since food has become cheaper to produce, restaurants can afford to give larger portions. No one has ever complained about receiving too much food, but everyone has complained about an unsatisfying dainty meal. In order to satiate everyone, restaurants began serving bigger portions, which started causing unneeded anxiety for those of us still in the Clean Plate Club. Whenever I'm at a restaurant and the server inevitably asks, "Are you finished with your meal?" offering to take my plate, it would just be easier to say, "Look into my eyes and when you see not a man, but a soulless monster who regrets every decision he has ever made, you'll know I'm finished."

"I... I can't... I might ralph..." I tell my wife, and honestly mean it. The busload of cookie dough did not receive a warm reception from the already-over-capacity food party in my stomach. With a twinge of guilt brought on by the knowledge there are kids starving in Africa, I toss the remaining two bites of the last cookie dough ball in the garbage along with my lifelong membership to the Clean Plate Club. We drag our feet like zombies toward a nearby park bench to recuperate from the physical and psychological repercussions of our latest State Fair indulgence.

I lean back on the bench, coasting into painful and forced heavy breathing like a woman in labor. The cookie dough settles into my stomach with the subtlety and charm of a dropped bowling ball. I never know my limit with food until I'm so far past it that it's out of my rearview mirror. I don't want to move again. Ever.

The State Fair is a hive of activity while I remain immobile on the bench, fearing that any movement could send food shooting out of an orifice. Workers mosey by with carts and supplies. Bustling around the corner from one of the food stands is a worker carrying a heaping bag of trash, the plastic on the verge of rupturing. As he walks by, a hole in his bag is spouting garbage juice—by far, the worst type of juice—like a rain gutter. Garbage juice is a collection of everything that is unwanted—everything you've thrown away, only now in liquid form! My mind replays the juice gushing from the bag onto the ground, where Fair goers stomp on it as they walk past oblivious. As repulsive as this is, it temporarily relieves me of the illness of deep regret from deep fried cookie dough.

Corn

I feel the "eating enough deep fried food to kill a circus elephant" nausea can be remedied with something healthy—a good, old fashioned vegetable. I head towards the stand selling grilled corn on the cob. Like most of the popular food stands at the State Fair, the corn on the cob stand is staffed by a dozen teenagers, swarming around the hut like little worker bees who exchanged honey for the sweet nectar of buttery corn on the cob. This is teamwork. No one is standing still. Everyone is aware of their specific purpose. It would be nice if life worked so efficiently.

I enter the line to exchange money for a ticket, and then shuffle into another line to exchange that ticket for corn on the cob. Both lines move quickly, and when I arrive at the corn stand, an adolescent and his wispy mustache greet me with genuine enthusiasm. I grin like an idiot as I hand him my ticket. This is the one time a year when I salivate in anticipation of a vegetable.

The young man, without turning, confidently hollers to his coworkers, "One corn!" His teenage peer snags a corn cob off the grill, peels back the husk, and briefly plunges the entire naked cob in a miniature hot tub of melted butter. Why have I never seen one of these butter baths anywhere else? If I had a tiny hot tub full of butter, I'd dip everything in it: chicken, fish, my head after a stressful day. I'd be dead in three days.

The cob re-emerges from the buttery hot tub, seductively dripping excess butter. The teen delicately hands me the corn as the butter soaks through all 5 napkins at the base of the cob. "Careful, it's hot," he warns, like someone informed him I burned my mouth on cheese curds today. As an adult, I don't need this warning. But as someone who eats with the patience of a child opening presents on Christmas morning, it is potentially life-saving.

As any foodie knows, buttered corn remains naked without salt. I approach the condiment area and hoist the cup of salt, with its tiny perforated air holes just big enough to let a few flakes through, and cautiously jiggle the salt onto my corn until I've arbitrarily decided that the salt level of my corn has reached perfection. Sinking my teeth into the corn, I recoil. "Wow, that is *hot!* Why did no one specifically warn me about this burning log of corn?," I exclaim to my wife. She nods in understanding, as if aware that this experience happens every year at the Fair.

Earlier this year I discovered a video on YouTube with an old man giving a tutorial on "cooking" corn in the microwave. He puts two ears of corn in the microwave, four minutes apiece. After eight minutes, he pulls them out, cuts off the fat end and the corn slithers right out of the shell. No pulling the hairs off the corn. No "shucking" as it's called. I replicated this experiment on my own with great success. Though as well as it worked for me, I still resent the fact that I'm using the microwave. Corn on the cob, like most food that needs to be cooked, does best on the grill, stovetop, or oven. Yet the ease and convenience of the microwave is so alluring I can't help but throw the corn in there and forget about it during the four sad minutes.

I take umbrage at the microwave since it's the lazy option and the one I most frequently resort to. If the goal is to eat food in its peak form, the microwave is never the best route. I only use it because a watched pot never boils and I don't trust my pots enough to boil my corn while I'm not watching. Also, my lack of patience plays a heavy role in opting for the microwave. The oven makes everything taste better, but when you're heating up a pre-made frozen meal, the goal isn't to savor the food, but to eat it and forget it. I hate the microwave, but maybe it's really that I hate my dependence on it.

Corn was meant to be grilled, which is why the State Fair makes me happy. Between bites of corn, I barely come up for air. Watching me eat corn this way is like watching an Olympic swimmer do the breaststroke—I'm moving so fast and with such fluid grace the mind can't even process it. Any witnesses to my eating just marvel at my graceful momentum.

"Whoa, you finished *already*?" my wife asks kindly. The pace at which I finish any food doesn't surprise her, but she likes to feign innocence. It's an endearing trait. I am a lucky man.

I discard my cob in the nearby trash. The beauty of corn is that it's delicious, yet only takes up a small percentage of stomach real estate, like pouring sand into a jar of rocks. I still have room to maneuver. As my wife finishes her corn in a distant second place, I acquire napkins to cleanse my hands of the buttery evidence, and bow my head in reverence (and sweep a few stray kernels off my shirt).

Thank you for everything, corn. You're one of my favorite enjoyments at the State Fair. I hope you never change.

Couples At The Fair

An entire family dressed in matching basketball jumpsuits hustles through the crowd like they're on a scavenger hunt. Watching them weave aerodynamically through the Minnesota masses makes me feel like a slob. Crossing their path is a young couple wearing matching Minnesota Gophers shirts.

The couples at the State Fair are one of a kind, with each person mirroring their significant other in the way they dress. The Minnesota State Fair is the Noah's Ark of people.

An elderly couple walk by, their heads garnished with safari hats. That is exactly what I want to be when I'm their age— someone who can confidently and casually wear a safari hat in public without fear of a passerby's snickering. They stroll leisurely side by side—close enough to enjoy each other's proximity, not so close they need to prove their companionship to anyone else with clasped hands or even make a statement about it to themselves, they are just comfortably themselves and a part of one another. They have a good life. No one who is unhappy with their life wears a safari hat in public.

Another couple proudly displays their Harley lifestyle. Dressed in this summer heat in matching leather chaps and bandanas, they remind me that I don't have the confidence to wear leather. I'd always be worried that someone would ask, "Why are you dressed up? It's not Halloween."

I notice the tattoos of the passing couples as well—if one person has a tattoo, the partner has one too. Did they have tattoos before, meeting through a conversation struck about the common ink they share? Or did they each get tattoos after becoming a couple? I fear too many things to get a tattoo, such as a typo or quitting halfway through because I couldn't handle the pain, only to be left with an incomplete tattoo for the rest of my life that reads, "I love" with the reader to ad-lib the rest (most likely with the word "farts"). Fortunately, my wife's skin is also devoid of any tattoos, especially ones that read "I love… (farts)" because she'd have to get one in order to match mine if we wanted to follow through with my State Fair theory about couples.

Flannel is an odd choice for such a hot day, but it is a joint decision of many couples at the State Fair. More practical and useful at the State Fair is a backpack accessory, which are things I see here in abundance here, but more specifically, in pairs. Rarely does only one half of a couple have a backpack. If one has a backpack, they both have a backpack. Perhaps because one person filled the backpack with things they wanted, thus causing the other to become jealous, wanting things of their own to bring along in their own backpack. This observation also regrettably applies to fanny packs, arguably one of the worst named products of all time (a close runner up to Ayds Diet Candy). "Fanny pack" sounds like the name of a product invented for obese kangaroos.

All of this is a reminder that we like people who are like us. We like to think opposites attract, but I don't see much evidence of that at the Fair, which I think is somewhat indicative of the population overall—as there are well over a million attendees every year. All this people watching seems to confirm my belief that what is similar is what attracts. We all drift toward the same side of our magnet.

My wife and I further prove this rule with our tattoo-less skin, fanny pack-less fannies, chapless legs and flannel-free bodies. But now we have a difference. I'm attracted to the promise of fun on the big yellow slide while she is cautious in rattling the hodgepodge of food we've ingested today. Differences are inevitable, you just have to hope that the force between you is strong enough to pull the other along for the ride as the distance grows. I set off on a quest, with wife trailing shortly behind, to live it up on the Giant Slide.

Giant Slide

Some moments in life require one to have the courage to be different and stand out. Whimsically flying down a giant plastic slide on a potato sack as a grown adult among children is one of them. I plop $2 on the counter, grab my ticket to childhood and hand it directly to another worker guarding the entrance five feet away.

I sling the potato sack over my shoulder and begin the long hike up what I lovingly call "Fun Mountain." The summit of the slide is about 1,000 feet tall. I'm not sure if that number is accurate, but I assume my gasping for breath is the result of a drastic altitude change and not a desperate cry for help from an overworked heart. As I sit at the top of the slide and begin to fashion my potato sack into a sled, two young boys around the age of 8 place their potato sacks next to me. Let the games begin, gentlemen.

"You can go," a young worker says, passively suggesting I make my way down the 170 foot slide. I give a courtesy nod to indicate I heard what he said, but fail to heed his command. I'm not pushing off until the two boys next to me push off. We're racing to the bottom whether they want to or not.

"It's all clear," the worker says, giving a second MinnePassive (Minnesota Passive) suggestion to get my cheeks down the slide and open up space at the top for a father and son to share a bonding experience.

Before the slide enforcer can once again imply the slide is as clear as a sunny day in July, the two kids push off, gliding down the slide at an aggressively slow pace. I shove off in my quest to the win the race they aren't aware we're having. As we hit the first mound on the wavy slide, the three of us are dead even. As I hit the second hump, for just a moment—a gloriously beautiful moment—I am weightless.

The entire duration at the State Fair, I've been constantly aware of how much I've eaten—always too much, while leaving room for just a little more food to force out the last remaining ounce of self-respect. On the slide, for a fleeting moment, I forget all of the guilt. The Papa Pup, cheese curds, corn on the cob, deep fried cookie dough—all weightlessly floating in my funhouse of a stomach. I'm liberated from lard, sailing toward the heavens on my... *Poof.* Back to being conscious of my sickeningly full stomach as the slide propels me far ahead of the two oblivious boys.

I coast to a halt at the bottom of the slide. I check my watch and let out an exaggerated yawn for the two kids who have run out of gas ten feet behind me. They don't notice my antics, but they don't feel wasted. This fun return to innocence was well-worth the price of admission, and watching the two boys run off the slide to enjoy other adventures reminds me why people have children—to be childlike again. There's the whole "continuing the human race" and "making the world a better place" reasons for children, but I think a big part of having kids must be acknowledging and wanting to experience the best of childhood again (only this time without fear of roller coasters). One cannot be angry while going down a slide. You will never see two people side by side on the giant slide arguing with each other. If foreign policy was hashed out on slides, the war in the Middle East would quickly simmer to the kind of tensions found only at a retirement home bingo game.

Basking in my landslide, I briefly consider another run down victory mountain, but I can't. Despite the thrill of coasting the waves of the slide, it's now obvious why I really craved the experience: For the vast majority of my time at the State Fair, I've been a slave to the food. Leaving my willpower at the entrance gate, I've been roaming the fairgrounds like a hungry hippo who never learned the words "I'm full." The slide presented my only opportunity at the Fair to feel in control. That's why I refused the passive aggressive nudge down the slide, that's why I felt so superior when I crushed my two weak competitors in our unofficial race to the bottom. For just a few great moments, I sailed above where my self-esteem has spent most of the day.

Alas, I'm far too gassed to voyage back up the endless flight of stairs. I'll settle for quietly enjoying my success at the bottom.

Largest Boar

Weaseling through the crowd at the swine barn, we finally catch a glimpse of what brought us here. Minnesota's Largest Boar, superfluously named Big Kenny, weighs in at a solid 1,045 pounds. It looks like a forklift dropped him there and he still hasn't mustered up the strength to get up to walk. Big Kenny has a long, thick body with disproportionately small legs that would look more natural on a coffee table than a half-ton animal. It's difficult to believe Big Kenny can even stand—his belly would just drag on the floor like an anchor.

As we all stare in shocked awe at Big Kenny, I get a sense we should be learning from this. Something other than that he has offensively large testicles, each roughly the size of a cantaloupe. I'm sure many parents had to uncomfortably explain those obscene nuts to their curious children who wondered if Big Kenny eats bowling balls. Only thirty seconds have passed, but I'm already getting the creeps.

What are we doing here, all of us? There are dozens of people gazing at Minnesota's Largest Boar. Big Kenny isn't spinning a beach ball on his snout, jumping through flaming hoops, or entertaining us behind a piano playing hits from the 80's. Big Kenny just lies sad on the hay like a beached whale.

Finally, it strikes me, the reason all of us are staring at Big Kenny: Whether we dare admit it or not, we are facing our darkest fears and lightest assurances. All of my behavior revolving food today—ALL of us and our treatment of deep fried consumables—could be described by any honest person as piggish. Big Kenny gives us comfort in letting us know that none of us are the fattest pig in the state, he is.

Big Kenny lets us pass judgments without a mirror to look back at ourselves. Big Kenny isn't here to entertain, but serve as the last refuge for a man desperate to distract himself from the guilt of eating too much food.

Big Kenny has a defeated look in his eye. Though Kenny has a tender sadness to him, today he is my hero—not the hero I wanted, but the hero I need—to wash away the deep fried guilt of excessive consumption. After a nod of respect to BK, I realize it's time to move on from this freak show to the circus of the The Mighty Midway.

Mighty Midway

The Mighty Midway features rides, attractions, carnival games, and the opportunity to prove one's worth as a human being by winning an oversized, stuffed Scooby Doo.

"Step right up! I'll guess ya age, I'll guess ya weight, I'll guess the month you were born! Fool the guesser! Any size, any prize!" shouts a small carnie, projecting his big voice with a blown out speaker as people stroll by in amusement. He has my attention with his bold psychic powers and, upon closer inspection, a set of choppers that could earn a dentist an early retirement. I don't know if I believe in the ability the carnie boasts, but I respect his bravado. There is a thin line between being willing to openly guess the weight or age of women and having a death wish. He treads that line like a drunk tight rope walker.

A quick glance at the prizes tells me everything I need to know about this gimmick: People aren't stepping in line in hopes of the man being wrong. All the prizes are nondescript stuffed animals, the kind so firm you'd swear it came from a taxidermy, not a toy factory. The kind of stuffed animal most often found hanging on the back of garbage trucks or, on a generous day, at the corner of suburban yards next to a sign scrawled, "FREE, PLEASE TAKE." For the participants, the prize is the carnie being wrong.

A young woman steps up to the plate, daring him to guess the month of her birth within two months. Clearly a much safer choice than asking him to guess her weight or age. I haven't read any scholarly studies to confirm this, but I've heard that age and weight may be sensitive subjects for a select fringe group of women who are concerned about their image. The man grins with the confidence of a magician about to perform his mental magic. It's now clear that he's missing a good 3 to 4 front teeth, all among the top row. Are the teeth missing due to a steady diet of cotton candy, or has he been repeatedly punched in the kisser by women after having erred on the plump side of the scale when guessing their weight?

The carnie scribbles his guess of her birth month on a small note pad, revealing it only to us bystanders as the woman in front of him waits patiently.

"When's your birthday, lady?" he asks.

"August," she says.

BAM!

"Look at that! Look at that, everyone! Incredible, just incredible," he says, nearly crushing his own back from patting it so hard.

"Who's next? Don't be shy now! Come on, come on," he says, with surprising charisma. Another woman approaches, challenging him to guess her weight.

"Ok, let's see here," he says, writing "142" on his notepad, again obscuring it from the participant, but showing it to the rest of us onlookers.

She steps on the scale, proving his guess to be 20 pounds too generous.

"Ohhhh, ok. Alright. Let's not show you that. You don't need to see that. Take ya prize, take ya prize..." he trails off, crumpling the paper before she can discover what he guessed, clearly intending to keep his remaining teeth. Because his guess of her weight was inaccurate, she's a winner at this game. But perception makes reality, and in reality he perceived her as twenty pounds heavier than she is. Who really won here?

I'm tempted to have him guess my weight. I honestly have no idea what it is. It's been over two years since I weighed myself. I was in a corporate building, searching the basement floor after hearing rumors of a vending machine living down there. Before I could discover the whereabouts of the vending machine, which I did, I stumbled upon an area that looked like an abandoned YMCA locker room from the 1970's, complete with creepy showers and an old fashioned medical weight scale. I don't remember what I weighed that day, but I remember getting peanut M&M's from the vending machine. My brain is a highly optimized machine that doesn't defeat itself by storing emotionally damaging data.

The appeal of having a professional guess your weight or age has to be that we all wonder what people really think of us. People generally view themselves overly harsh while others are overly kind. Because of this dichotomy, we never really have an accurate picture of ourselves. For the small fee of just two tickets, we are offered the chance to receive honesty we otherwise can't afford.

An Asian woman walks up and asks him to guess her age. "I don't have a damn clue. Just go ahead and claim ya prize," he says. Or that's what I would have said if I were him to save everyone time. There is no group of people whose age is harder to guess than Asian women. They look youthful well into their glory years while the rest of us wrinkle, resembling a person who spent their entire life in a bathtub.

He holds up his guess to the peanut gallery revealing a middle-of-the-road guess of 28 years old.

I wouldn't be surprised if she were 18 or 40. I'm not sure if it has to do with diet, good genetics, or if Asian women have access to a secret youth preserving elixir, but whatever it is, it works.

"How old are ya, darling?" he asks.

"Twenty-one," she says, smiling before knowing his guess, as if she's been on a multi-state tour humiliating carnies.

The husband walks over to us, "I've gotta ask. How old did he think she was?"

"Twenty-eight," I tell him.

"You see, I'm thirty-one and she's twenty-one so I could see why he'd think that. He probably looked at me and thought we were both older," he explains to me.

The woman proudly selects a disposable stuffed animal while the sales pitch continues with no enthusiasm lost, "I'll guess ya age. I'll guess ya weight. I'll guess the month of your birthday." People keep funneling in, but we decide to move on. He's a one trick pony.

We walk a circle around the carnie games and rides before walking out of the Midway, continuing our people watching elsewhere at the Fair. Due to the contents still churning in my stomach, we opt against a ride before we leave. I need one of those motorized scooters a handful of people ride around in at the State Fair, granting me an effortless way to leisurely roam the fairgrounds while having the option to terrorize the heels of any patrons who don't heed their motorized authority.

My wife and I pass a booth selling ¼ pound slices of bacon served on a stick. In line is a man wearing noise-canceling headphones. Strangely, the man's headphones are the first thing I noticed, not the yard stick-sized bacon on display. I'm so full, I'm beyond the point of being seduced by bacon porn.

What could he *possibly* be listening to? The headphones give off the impression he arrived at the State Fair with only one purpose—to devour bacon. Any chit chat or other human interaction outside of the necessary exchange to obtain bacon is obviously frowned upon—strange, since he made such effort to be here, an event known as "The Great Minnesota Get-Together." I find this so unusual, until a horrific stench awakens my sense—someone's rancid body odor.

Sweet Martha's Cookies, where is that foul body odor coming from? This is the first time I've smelled another human today and it's surprisingly more unpleasant than the random stink of horse manure. With manure, there's only one shade of smell. Humans are endlessly inventive in discovering new ways to assault nostrils. Who is the source of this mishmash of sweat, grease, and a stubborn refusal to shower? Clearly a man! Women are too self-aware to not know when they reek, while men often need to be prodded like cattle into taking a shower (the exception to this is rule is the entire country of France).

Crazy people are starting to appear. At the nearby Spin-a-Painting (a booth where customers—or, more aptly, their children who have convinced their parents that their refrigerator door needs new artwork—can create something magical by splattering paint onto a canvas), a man in a ponytail sporting cutoff jean shorts leans in to watch children work on their creations. He has one leg propped upon a small bench meant for children to stand on, his thigh sprawled as if in the middle of a pre-marathon stretch. The red flag he's raising burns brighter than that of a Spanish bullfighter yelling "Toro! Toro! Toro!"

Similar to the sun, one can't stare at a male leg for more than a few seconds without risking permanent blindness. This man's decision to wear thigh high shorts—and to display them so proudly—has left an image in my mind that can only be washed away by more food, specifically a strawberry milkshake. My wife and I move toward the Dairy Barn with a renewed sense of urgency.

Milkshake

Hustling in pursuit of the Dairy Barn for a milkshake, all motion halts as my right flip flop refuses to join my leg in the forward stride.

"Oh… sorry..." a middle aged man says, quickly liberating my flip flop from the pressure of his shoe. I scowl at the man, but deep down, I know the fault is mine.

I like to think I'm somewhat smart, or am at least capable of being smart in brief flashes. Sure, I'll never crank out a solution to complex math problems while roaming the halls of MIT during my night shift as a janitor, but I didn't chug glue and eat paint chip sandwiches for lunch as a kid, so I'm not exactly thick in the head either.

By wearing flip flops (the cheap version of sandals) to the State Fair, I'm challenging the notion I'm not a doofus. Flip flops are great to wear to the beach, but that's about it. When you wear flip flops to the beach, the audible flipping and flopping is mostly muted by the sand. As I was walking into the State Fair, it echoed off the concrete, generating a sound only slightly less annoying than a squawking crow on caffeine pills.

Every single time I've worn flip flops to a mass gathering, they've been stomped on well into the double digits. There is never any need to walk that close to someone, even if you're following them out of a burning building. And the icing on the flip flop cow pie is that my feet will be covered in all types of gross dirt by the end of the day. For all I know, the old man just spent the day carelessly stepping in horse turds. Now I worry each time my heel connects with the flip flop, it's meshing with secondhand manure.

All of this flip flop suffering is for the simple pleasure of enabling my feet to breathe, which is almost never worth the payment of foot stomping. I feel as though there is a whole underground society of flip flop stompers roaming the earth in search of the fool who dares to force upon the world their hideous feet. Why? I know that every time I wear flip flops in public, my feet get stomped upon. Not just once. Not just twice. Countless times. Countless.

Nothing makes sense about how most people dress for the State Fair, my decisions included. I should have selected an old pair of shoes, ones demoted to only being worn while mowing the lawn. This contemplation is cut short by a voice screaming above the dull roar of the crowd.

"DO YOU EVEN KNOW THE MEANING OF THE WORD 'NO?!'" an angry parent yells. The child doesn't answer, likely due to embarrassment and not the awareness of the question being rhetorical. My instinct is to cast judgment, but who is to say I'd be any better? Anyone who isn't a parent (and I'm not, even though I look 9 months pregnant with a food baby) can't judge parents with 100% credibility, as they haven't walked a mile in their flip flops.

I'd like to say I'd be patient with my children, but in five years, I might become everything I have seen, and I'll be the guy walking my kid around on a leash, barking at him to pump the breaks on the mini donuts because we agreed to split them 50/50 (which means I get to eat 80% of them).

It's easy to look at this mom and say that she needs to get her anger in control, but maybe the kid should also be on trial. He's not contributing to the household income (e.g., working long hours in a factory or coal mine), in fact, he's depleting limited resources from it. He probably has public meltdowns frequently. Each meltdown likely displays the kind of reaction he should reserve for receiving news that his entire family died in a terrible car accident on the way to Disneyland. But in reality, the cause of his disturbance is that his mom (who is alive and well) told him he couldn't have deep fried Oreos because he's already eaten his weight in fried food at the Fair, sending him into this escalating end-of-the-world tantrum.

So when the kid is demanding to eat every sugar-stuffed food in sight, go on every single ride that will make him throw up the food he just ate, and wants to be carried instead of walking, it's understandable his mom has some built up tension that has to be released by emotive yelling. It's also possible the child is a sadist and was asking if he could step on a stranger's flip flops, and the mom is my unsung hero.

The kid hovers on the edge of tears as his mom grips his hand and disappears into the crowd. I flip flop onto the Dairy Barn. The sweet smell that is a mix of manure and barn alerts me that we're getting close. This unique odor isn't repulsive, it is connected to the best milkshakes in the state—it makes me believe in the authenticity of the dairy products used, and that the wholesome ingredients is to account for why the milkshakes are so amazing.

As if playing a game of hopscotch, I step carefully across the street littered with fresh horse droppings. Finally, after this long pilgrimage, we've arrived at the Dairy Barn. Right outside the entrance to the Dairy Barn (a safe enough distance from the random bacteria from cows inside the barn), is a little milkshake stand serving chocolate, vanilla, and strawberry shakes. The only bad decision is indecision.

The line is moving quickly with people not needing time to consider their selection.

We inch forward as the older man in front of us asks the cashier with a straight face, "Do you have malts?" Absurd. What is there to like about a malt? A malt is a shake that's been vandalized by manufactured powder. A shake is pure, and elegantly simple. The malt was originally invented as a nutritional supplement for infants. I've never enjoyed malt flavoring just like I don't enjoy snacking on carrot puree and creamed peas. The shake need not be sabotaged with some infant powder that only taints the simple joy only a milkshake can deliver.

I hand the cashier exact change for a strawberry shake and in the same minute the clouds part, angels sing, and a strawberry milkshake descends from the heavens into my hand. I seal my lips around the straw and summon the strawberry shake to the back of my throat. The anticipation surges as the cool drink shimmies up the straw. And then nirvana. The simplest form of a dessert hits that nostalgic spot that reverberates throughout my entire body. I don't care that I can smell fresh cow manure or that the man in front of me tried to push his malt agenda at the State Fair. This is a perfect moment.

"Slow down," my wife pleads, taking control of the vanishing milkshake. As if one would leave by choice after entering the gates of heaven. The milkshake hugs every single morsel of food in my stomach I've consumed so far.

My wife marches the milkshake close to the finish line, handing it off in an unspoken agreement that I will drain the shake to empty. In our relationship, we've never explicitly come to this agreement or verbalized it, but I'm like a food hitman. Whenever she can't quite get the job done, whether it's due to hitting her limit for a certain food or ridiculous portion sizes, the food is passed off to me. I consume and erase all evidence the food ever existed, ensuring that if our parents were watching remotely, we would be in the Clean Plate Club.

We wander without purpose with the remaining milkshake. There's some force guiding me around the Fair—it may be my subconscious trying to burn a few calories.

There's now only a little left of my milkshake. I'm only able to access it if I'm willing to indulge everyone within 30 feet of me with heavy straw slurping—which I do, as I walk around in my flip flops. The combination of the slurping and flip flop noises makes me a frontrunner for Most Annoying Person at the Fair. There's no sympathy from anyone I pass. The look on their faces read, "It's gone. Give up. There's nothing left you can do." I pump that straw like an emergency room doctor performing CPR on a patient he refuses to accept has passed.

Finally, long after it should occur, I am resigned to the truth: It's time to move on. I drop my empty milkshake cup in one of the thousands of garbage receptacles and embark upon our next adventure.

Miracle of Birth

Inside the Miracle of Birth Center, I get to witness one of the most grotesque acts as well as one of the most beautiful. Everything in baby form is cute, yet the birth process is a screaming, pain-filled adventure. Most of the miracle is that something so cute could erupt from such torturous chaos. If my views on the birthing process seem hyperbolic, you'll have to understand that the moment I entered this world, my Dad fainted against the hospital wall, sliding toward the ground in slow motion until his head was crudely caught by a trash can.

A mix between circus and hospital, the center stage becomes surrounded by crowds of kids and parents patiently snacking, waiting for a cow in labor to bring her baby calf into this troubled world. I don't want to see this. I know the baby calf will be adorable, but why witness it if you don't have to? One wrong glance at a calf seeing the world for the first time will trigger a vomit montage of all the food I've eaten today. Pregnant women should never get in an unreliable elevator with me.

The Birth Center appears more crowded than any other building at the Fair, causing me to change from normal walking to side-shuffling in attempt to navigate the area for a cute baby animal to pet. I come upon a teenager holding a baby pig out to adoring children, all with outstretched hands and big grins. I take in the presence of this adorable piglet while trying not to think about how much bacon I eat on a weekly basis.

The teenager answers questions about the pig in her arms and informs us that the animal is just 3 days old. I lean forward to cautiously pet the little critter. The teen asks if there are any other questions and I have to refrain from asking if people have pigs as pets, like in the movie *Babe*. It requires further willpower to restrain myself from uttering a proud but stoic, "That'll do, pig. That'll do."

Holding the pig might ruin bacon for me, which is just the same as ruining my life. Snoozing in the arms of its teen caretaker, the piglet is ridiculously adorable and content while bunches of strangers rub their greasy mitts on him. He probably won't grow up to skip the butcher for a life of sheep herding in competitions like in the movies, but that's the story I'm going to tell myself today. That's how I get by in life, weaving intricate narratives to wash away the food-induced guilt. With that, I realize I've had all I can take of the State Fair for this year. That'll do, Ben. That'll do.

A Brief Visit To The Restroom

Like any normal person, I prefer using my own bathroom to a public one. Waiting until I'm back home would mean waiting another 35 - 45 minutes, as that is how long the bus ride could be—perhaps even longer if the public transportation breaks down, which happens occasionally. Realizing it is best to simply use the facilities before exiting the fair, I muster the courage to journey into the barbaric wasteland known as The Public Restroom.

I enter the restroom and find myself in the middle of a flurry of activity. Kids clap their sticky hands at the sink where their dads remind them to "focus" and "For the love of God, just wash your hands." Paper towels are discarded across the floor like tumbleweed blown across an abandoned town, and my flip flops squish beneath me, skidding on liquid that I can't call "water" with any degree of certainty.

I soldier forward, trying to make my way past the stalls over to the urinal. As I pass a closed stall, a man—or possibly a demonic beast—punishes my ears with what sounds like a kid with a collapsing lung playing the tuba. It is at this point I decide to skip the urinal. I walk back to my wife, announcing that I'd much rather spend another 45 minutes risking an exploding bladder trying to get home to pee in the comfort of our own home than risk the psychological trauma of spending another moment in the State Fair public restroom.

Leaving The Fair

My wife and I stumble exhausted towards the exit, feet no longer rising ambitiously into the air with each stride. They now drag forward in a zombie like stroll. Fresh-faced fairgoers breeze by us on their way in, while a mosquito begins extracting blood from my neck. Do I have enough energy to swat the world's worst insect? I slap my neck in slow motion only to watch the mosquito fly away with my blood and type 2 diabetes from all the sugar I consumed today.

After what seems like hours of walking, we come upon a bus, which shines like a beacon of light in my weary haze. My wife and I enter, nod towards the driver as a silent communication of "Hey," and find a seat towards the middle of the half empty bus. I realize what a relief it is to be seated again.

Every sensory input in my brain is fried from consumption, over-stimulation, and/or fatigue. Despite my wish to not exert any further energy, my mind wanders, and I again ponder the question of "Why do I come here?

I thought the conclusion I'd arrive at would be that the State Fair isn't just a masochistic eating spree, but an opportunity to bond and be surrounded by people just like me. There are many self-centered reasons for one to go to the State Fair, but deep down, we crave the communal element. Strangely, eating grotesque amounts of food by ourselves would be more sad than surrounding ourselves with the crowd at the State Fair. Maybe that's why we all come here.

Arriving here on the bus this morning, I had no real purpose except to enjoy a few items that I can only savor at the State Fair. With a clear beginning and end, my time was limited so I made the most of it by experiencing as much as possible. The tragedy of the State Fair, as well as life in general, is that while you can experience anything you want, you never have the time, money, or stomach to experience *everything*.

I relieved the joys of childhood on the Giant Slide while by racing two children to the bottom. It was there that I realized why people have children, and it is to experience this much excitement in everyday life. I critiqued the couples at the State Fair for being a replica of their significant other, only to realize that my wife and I are no different. I sought out the largest boar in Minnesota so I could feel superior to something for once in the day, but left feeling worse. The miracle of birth horrifies me, yet I loved the result of the little piglet. I came to the State Fair to observe others, yet in everyone else I found a mirror reflecting something back about myself.

Life, it seems, is a continuum with the capability to experience either end of an emotion at any time. The State Fair is my yearly reminder of what it is to be alive, to make the most of the short time we have, and to experience as much as possible before it all ends—even if that means scorching the roof of your mouth on deep fried cheese curds.

What brings me to the State Fair is not just cravings for food, but a hunger for life.

I'll be back next year.

About The Author

Ben Nesvig is a writer, cupcake connoisseur, participation trophy winner (4th grade track and field relay race), bacon chef, failed vacuum salesman, and author of two books. His first book is *First World Problems: 101 Reasons Why The Terrorists Hate Us*.

For extra content that wasn't included in the book, visit http://mnstatefairbook.com

Connect with Ben

Twitter:
@BenNesvig

Email:
Hi@bennesvig.com

Did you enjoy your read? Be Minnesota Nice and leave a review on Amazon.

Made in the USA
San Bernardino, CA
26 June 2015